IMAGES OF ENGLAND

BUXTON AND THE HIGH PEAK
FROM THE BOARD COLLECTION

IMAGES OF ENGLAND

BUXTON AND THE HIGH PEAK
FROM THE BOARD COLLECTION

MIKE BENTLEY, MIKE LANGHAM
AND COLIN WELLS

TEMPUS

Frontispiece: Buxton's town centre after a fall of snow in around 1955.

First published 2006

Tempus Publishing Limited
The Mill, Brimscombe Port,
Stroud, Gloucestershire, GL5 2QG
www.tempus-publishing.com

© Mike Bentley, Mike Langham and Colin Wells, 2006

British Library Cataloguing in Publication Data.
A catalogue record for this book is available from the British Library.

ISBN 0 7524 3951 0

Typesetting and origination by Tempus Publishing Limited.
Printed in Great Britain.

Contents

Acknowledgements

We want to thank those who have helped with this publication. Firstly, the Derbyshire County Council, Libraries and Museum Service, who have given permission for us to reproduce the images in this book. All the photographs except the family pictures have been taken from the Board Collection held at the Buxton Museum and Art Gallery. We are grateful to Ros Westwood, the curator, and the staff of the museum for their unfailing help, also the staff at the Buxton Library local studies department for providing such an excellent service. A number of people have helped us with captioning and other information, they are: Gordon Ashmore, Tom and Elaine Bagguley, Robert Cooke, Jack Ford, Betty Jackson, Steve King, Barbara Langham, Margaret Lomas, David Ripley, Arthur Robinson, Dorothy Wells. We thank them all.

M.J.L, C.W., J.M.B.,
Buxton, Spring 2006

Above: J.R. Board seated in the centre with John Meddins to his left and staff of Watsons of Sheffield.

Left: John Davis Meddins in later life.

Introduction

The first volume of Buxton from the Board Collection was well received and our publishers asked us to compile a further selection of photographs for a second volume. It has been a great pleasure to revisit the half-plate glass negatives, now safely catalogued and boxed in the Buxton Museum and Art Gallery, and to view again this unique collection of twentieth-century life in Buxton and places around. In volume one we selected images of Buxton and its immediate vicinity, but in this second volume we follow the firm of J.R. Board out and about on assignments in some of the towns and villages in the High Peak, as well as in Buxton. So we look at nearby towns of Whaley Bridge and Chapel-en-le-Frith, and we follow the photographer to some of the High Peak villages, such as: Monyash, Litton, Hurdlow, Taddington, Tideswell and Great Longstone. And we have sought to present a wide range of activities to give a very real flavour of the sheer diversity of assignments undertaken by the firm. Thus we record road haulage and motor garages at Chapel-en-le-Frith, egg grading and packing in Great Longstone, an artificial insemination unit and ex-War Department vehicle conversion in Fairfield, and quarrying and limestone manufacture, post-war engineering, banking and retail business in the Peak District.

But most of the work of this firm was carried out in Buxton, a spa town high in the hills of the Peak District, which has attracted visitors through time. From Roman times the town has welcomed visitors and its history is rich with accounts of visits by the aristocracy and wealthy coming to take the waters for their health. It enjoyed great popularity in late medieval times when Mary Queen of Scots visited to take the waters on five occasions between 1573 and 1584 and brought in her trail important members of the Elizabethan court, including the Earl of Leicester, and Lord Burghley, the Lord Treasurer. Buxton was developed as a Georgian spa by the fifth Duke of Devonshire who commissioned the architect, John Carr of York, to design a magnificent crescent, new baths and stables between 1780 and 1789. But its heyday was reached in the nineteenth century when Buxton became a health resort to rival Harrogate and Bath. The nineteenth and early twentieth centuries saw phenomenal growth of population, accommodation and medicinal facilities in the town and many people came to take the waters and receive hydrotherapy and associated treatments for their ailments. In 1905, at the height of Buxton's fame as a spa, King Edward VII and Queen Alexandra visited and toured all the amenities. This reputation continued into the early part of the twentieth century, though the development of the town was, inevitably, shaped by two world wars and, as interest in water medicine declined, Buxton had to reinvent itself as an inland resort and conference centre. The development of J.R. Board's business coincided with this twentieth-century reshaping of the town, so we are able to record visual memories of Buxton as a conference town, presenting its amenities to the visitor, taking leisure in its parks and gardens, being educated, enjoying its celebrities both visitor and resident, and coping with the winter weather.

The firm of J.R. Board at 9 Cavendish Circus remained a household name for photography right through the mid-twentieth century, but it was preceeded in Buxton by a number of commercial photographers, beginning with a pioneer from the early days of photography, Barrowclough Wright Bentley, who established his studio in town in 1851. As the technology rapidly developed, others set up in business including B.W. Bentley's cousin, William Bentley, and his successor John Hobbis. By the end of the century others, such as: D.C. Latham of Station Road, Professor Simpson and Arundel Hall in Spring Gardens, and W. G. Hosler in the Quadrant, were making a living in the town. In 1911, Robert Forgy Hunter established a photographic shop and studio at Grafton House, No. 1 the Quadrant. R.F. Hunter quickly forged a reputation, opening a new American electric studio under the direction of Mr E.C. Iliffe, late of W.W. Winter Photography, Derby. Soon after the firm was established, Hunter also took on a young photographer by the name of James Robert Board. By 1916 the business had moved to 9 Cavendish Circus with darkroom premises in the Old Court House, George Street.

An advertisement for
Board's of Buxton.

J.R. Board originated from Sheffield where he had worked and probably trained under a
photographic firm called Watsons. He moved to Buxton in the early part of the twentieth century,
continuing his photographic career with Hunters, and, when R.F. Hunter left to further his
fortunes in London, J.R. Board took over the business. From 1926, Board's Buxton business was
very successful and he quickly gained a reputation for quality which attracted such worthies to his
studio as David Lloyd George, George Bernard Shaw and the family of the dukes of Devonshire, to
be the subjects of his portraiture. As a commercial photographer Board's work covered a large range
of subjects, from townscape, events, publicity, advertising, commerce, portraiture, postcards and many
general scenes of life in Buxton and the High Peak.

J.R. Board, when not behind the camera lens or in the darkroom, had a range of interests which
included zoology and history. He was born in 1888 and served for four years with the Royal
Engineers in the First World War, and it was during this time that he was quite severely gassed, an
incident which was thought to have contributed to his relatively early death at the age of fifty-four.
He was a Conservative by political persuasion and was a member of the Constitutional Club. His
wife, Elizabeth, was sixteen years older than he and they did not have any children, but she had a
son, John, by a previous marriage. Elizabeth had her own drapery shop at 49 High Street, Buxton,
and despite her marriage to Board, traded under her first married name of Meddins. John was also
involved in photography from an early age. Born in Buxton in 1900 he was brought up in Byron
Street and educated at Kents Bank school. At fifteen he went to work as a photographer's assistant
for W.G. Hosler, gaining experience in darkroom work, printing, developing and enlarging for three
years before enlisting in the army. He joined his stepfather, J.R. Board, during the time of Hunter's
business in Buxton and they worked together until Board died in 1943. John Davis Meddins took
over the firm from that time but still continued to trade under the name of Boards of Buxton, a
name which had by then become synonymous with quality. The retirement of Meddins in around
1968 brought about another change of ownership when business was taken over by Roy Turner,
who continued under the same trading name until his retirement in about 1980. On Turner's
retirement the business was wound up.

Over more than forty years, Board and his stepson, John Meddins, produced a large collection
of photographs using old-style half-plate cameras. The collection of glass negatives at the Buxton
Museum and Art Gallery has been catalogued by the authors of this book. For those wishing to
delve further into the collection, a good selection of the images have been scanned onto the *Picture
the Past* website. This is operated by the libraries and museums of Derby, Derbyshire, Nottingham
and Nottinghamshire, and includes hundreds of thousands of historic photographs, slides, negatives,
glass plates, postcards and engravings, recalling the history of the local communities over the last
hundred years and more. The address is www.picturethepast.org.uk.

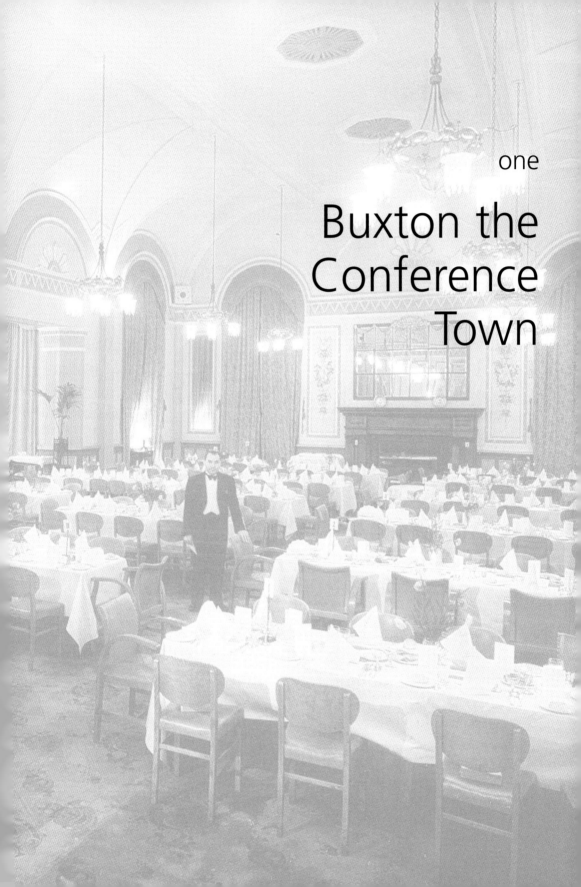

one

Buxton the Conference Town

After the First World War the popularity of the spa and hydropathic movement dipped and Buxton repositioned itself as a conference centre, a resource it was able to offer right through the mid-twentieth century. Conferences for national bodies such as the County & Municipal Engineers, the National Meat Federation and the Liberal Party were held in town. J.R. Board took photographs of the conferences and the hotels for publicity brochures. In this chapter we show a sample of the firm's commercial work, which gives a flavour of how the visitor was accommodated in town. The picture above appeared in a Buxton conference brochure of 1935 and is an artist's impression of the ballroom at the Palace Hotel.

The Palace Hotel, opened in 1868, stands near the railway station and overlooks the town as one of Buxton's most prominent hotels.

Part of the Cavendish Restaurant at the Palace Hotel in March 1963.

The Sun Lounge at the Palace Hotel in 1931, with the fashionable cane furniture of the time.

A large function room at the Palace Hotel set for conference dining and supervised here by the head waiter in January 1935.

The Palace Hotel has a fitness suite and swimming pool. Here the swimming pool is shown in typical decor of 1939.

Right: The Old Hall Hotel has offered hospitality to the traveller since 1573. Throughout its long history, additions and improvements have been made and today the hotel is somewhat larger than the Derbyshire square house of its medieval origin. To quote the hotel's website, 'the interesting and famous still eat, drink and sleep within its mellowed walls'.

Below: The Old Hall Hotel in about 1948 with very trendy window blinds!

The Old Hall Hotel's most famous guest was Mary Queen of Scots, who stayed on seven occasions between 1573 and 1584 whilst the prisoner of Queen Elizabeth I. Her gaoler was the Sixth Earl of Shrewsbury, who was married to Derbyshire's Bess of Hardwick. Here is the Shrewsbury Room in the hotel set for a conference dinner.

In this photograph J.R. Board has managed to obscure the Old Hall Hotel with a tree! But the image, taken in 1933, is redolent of the conference town of the period. On the left is the Pavilion Gardens, a well-used conference venue, and the tower of St John's church can be seen in the background.

In the Pavilion Gardens the large concert hall, known as the Octagon, could accommodate up to 2,000 delegates. Here is a conference in the 1930s.

Adjacent to the large concert hall were lounges where conference delegates could relax between sessions. The Pavilion Gardens, being of iron and glass and facing south, offered splendid suntraps, one of which is seen here in around 1930.

Conference dining arrangements in the Pavilion Gardens in October 1964.

THE SPA HOTEL · BUXTON

On New Year's Day, 1931, the Buxton Hydro Hotel on Hartington Road changed its name to the Spa Hotel, in order to reflect the changing nature of its clientele and its increasing use as a conference venue. H.R.P. Lomas, who ran the hotel for many years, was a very astute publicist and here J.R. Board has photographed an artist's impression in February 1933, which gives a very fashionable view of the hotel.

At the Spa Hotel in May 1938, when the visitor could look forward to a very cosy bedroom warmed by a coal fire.

Many chefs were employed at the Spa Hotel to serve up to 230 guests in the dining room. For special conference dinners it was quite usual for the chefs to display their culinary creations, and here is a presentation buffet set out in June 1946.

Milton House on Broad Walk was built in 1864 and was always run as a private lodging house or hotel. In the mid-twentieth century it was owned by H.R.P. Lomas and used as additional accommodation for the Spa Hotel.

The Grove Hotel on the corner of Spring Gardens has its origins as a Georgian coffee house. The property dates to the early 1770s and had later enlargements. This view was taken in 1937.

The lounge in the Grove Hotel in 1937 reflects its earlier 'olde worlde' charm.

The writing room of the Grove Hotel in 1937. It is now the dining room.

In the 1930s it was possible to motor into the centre of a town and have your car taken to the hotel garage for the duration of your stay. Here is the Grove Hotel Garage in 1937 with some splendid examples of automobile marques of the time.

The St Ann's Hotel formed part of the magnificent Georgian Crescent and operated continuously from 1788 until closure in 1989. This view was taken in about 1938 and shows a quiet, uncluttered forecourt. It will be noticed that the Pump Room to the left has no corner domes: these were taken down in 1937. Conservation plans for 2006 onwards will see a new thermal spa hotel in the crescent with the Natural Baths, seen at the very rear of this picture, transformed for modern spa and wellness treatments. The Pump Room with new corner domes will become a coffee house where it will also be possible to drink Buxton Natural Thermal Mineral Water as in times past.

A lounge at St Ann's Hotel in June 1936. Though modified through the years, original Georgian features can be seen in this photograph in the architraved doorway to the right and the Italianate window with deep panelled reveal to the left.

The Brunswick Hotel on Hardwick Square East was built in 1877-8. It is pictured here in April 1938, with the hotel's own taxi parked outside.

From the mid-1950s the Brunswick Hotel became a conference centre, operated by Derbyshire County Council and known as the Derbyshire Conference House. This continued the Buxton conference tradition into the 1970s when this photograph was taken. It is now known as Charis House, a faith-based organisation providing accommodation and a nursery.

The George Hotel in The Square, seen here in September 1937, was managed by William Nall and catered for functions in its large café and restaurant.

The proprietors survey the table layout set for a wedding reception at the George Hotel in September 1938.

Here is the light and airy George Hotel dining room ready to serve mid-morning coffee or a light lunch in December 1936.

The Savoy Hotel, formerly The Burlington, in addition to offering accommodation, also had two popular bars where the conference delegates could relax in the evenings. Here is the popular Spanish Bar.

The cellar bar at the Savoy Hotel was known as The Hole in the Wall. It became a popular haunt for locals in the 1960s.

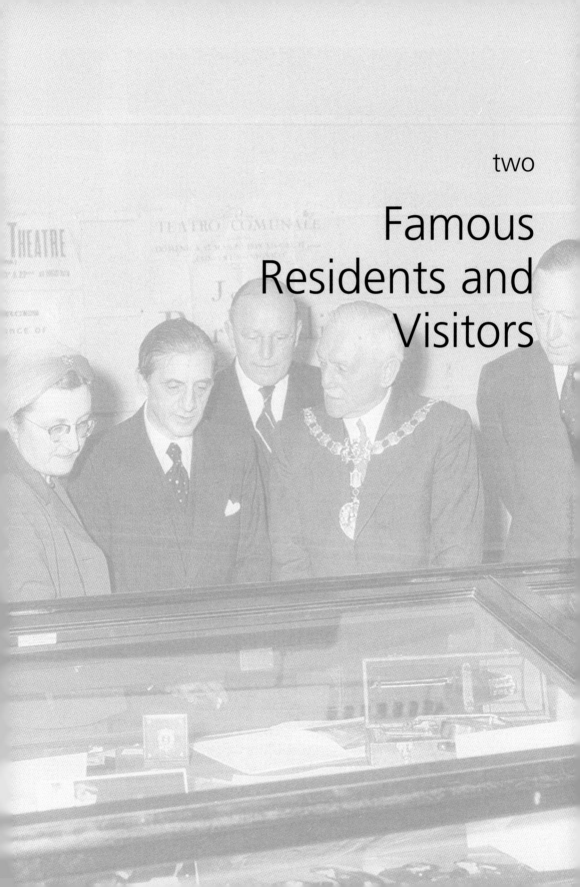

two

Famous Residents and Visitors

Many famous people have visited Buxton and the High Peak including members of royalty and the aristocracy. The theatre tradition, developed from the early part of the twentieth century, saw famous actors in Buxton for appearances on stage, and the conference years welcomed notable politicians and others. Add to this some of the characters in the area and J.R. Board can present in this chapter a pot pourri of prominent people. This image shows the actors Douglas Fairbanks Senior and Mary Pickford outside the Palace Hotel Buxton in 1924. They were in town to prepare for the film *Dorothy Vernon of Haddon Hall,* in which Miss Pickford played Dorothy Vernon.

Opposite above: In the Municipal Year 1919/20 the Right Hon. The Marquis of Hartington, later tenth Duke of Devonshire, was the mayor of Buxton. Here he is seen giving a speech in Buxton.

Opposite below: The ninth Duke of Devonshire with the Revd Canon C.E. Scott-Moncrieff, Vicar of Buxton, outside St John's church in about 1920.

Right: In the early 1930s the Liberal Party held their annual conference at Buxton. Here is David Lloyd George (1863-1945), former Liberal Prime Minister. After the First World War, in which he took a powerful leadership position, presiding over a war cabinet of five politicians, he spent five months in Paris negotiating the peace treaty and working to seek peace and economical survival in Europe. This culminated in the Genoa Conference of 1922. Presiding over a falling membership, he worked hard as chairman of the parliamentary party to restore liberalism. From this time he continued to campaign for progressive causes, but without a political party to support him, he was never to hold power again. During the 1920s, Lloyd George produced several reports on how Britain could be improved, including 'We Can Conquer Unemployment' (1929).

Below: The Right Hon. The Marquis of Hartington speaking with his father, the ninth Duke of Devonshire, outside the Pump Room at Buxton in 1920. To the left of the picture may be seen the Town Clerk wearing a legal wig and Geneva tabs, and further to his left the Revd Canon C.E. Scott-Moncrieff, Vicar of Buxton.

Right: In 1926 the Buxton Corporation bought the Pavilion Gardens from the Buxton Gardens Company for £29,550. The twenty-strong municipal orchestra in the gardens was conducted by Horace Fellowes from 1928 to 1935.

Below: In 1937 the orchestra at the Pavilion Gardens was known as the Buxton Spa Orchestra. It played for tea dances (*thé dansants*) in the afternoon and gave evening concerts. The conductor was Maurice Miles.

The Buxton International Festival of Music ran every year from 1959 for almost ten years, and it always featured the Halle Orchestra. In the opening year, a tribute to Sir John Barbirolli, who had been with the Halle since 1943, was presented at the Buxton Library and Museum on Terrace Road. Here Sir John Barbirolli is viewing the exhibition with the Mayor and Mayoress of Buxton, Cllr and Mrs Edward Hawley.

Sir John Barbirolli, conductor of the Halle Orchestra, speaking in the large concert hall at the Buxton and North Derbyshire Festival of Music in 1961.

Messrs Advent Hunstone of Tideswell were a long-established firm of wood carvers: their work can be seen in Tideswell Church. Advent Hunstone was a fine artist, as can be seen from these drawings. This is of St John the Baptist Tideswell and the adjacent George Inn, for a Christmas card in 1958.

Advent Hunstone made this drawing of the historic Glee Club at Tideswell, attended in the eighteenth century by Samuel Slack, a wonderfully sonorous bass singer who became famous, giving concerts all over the country. But Samuel Slack never forgot his roots, and he liked nothing more than to sing over a mug of ale with his friends in Tideswell. He is buried in the small graveyard on the north side of the church and his stone is engraved *'Gloria Deo, as a tribute of respect to the memory, musical taste, talent and vocal powers of Samuel Slack. This stone was erected by the voluntary contributions of the Barlow choir and a few other admirers of that noble deep-toned melodist, who died August 10th 1822 aged 65 years'.*

George Bernard Shaw (1856-1950), the playright and critic, visited town during the time of the Buxton Old Vic Drama festivals. The first festival in 1937 presented Shaw's play *Pygmalion,* directed by Tyrone Guthrie. J.R. Board was proud to have taken the portrait of a man described as *'the greatest playright in the English language of the twentieth century'.*

Alec Guinness played the title role in *Hamlet* at the second Buxton Old Vic Drama Festival which ran from 29 August to 17 September 1938. Seen here in Buxton at the age of twenty-four, he acted alongside other well-known names, including Andrew Cruikshank and Anthony Quayle.

The actor Emlyn Williams signed to work for the Old Vic as he was on the point of signing a contract to go to Hollywood. So he appeared in Buxton playing Angelo in Shakespeare's *Measure for Measure,* and Oswald in *Ghosts,* by Henrik Ibsen, at the Buxton Festival of 1937.

Anthony Hawtry (1909-54) was the actor/manager who brought a repertory company to the Buxton Playhouse in the late 1940s and early 1950s. The company featured many now well-known actors, including Nigel Hawthorne, Patrick Cargill, Gwen Watford and Jos Ackland. Another member of the company, Shaun Sutton, went on to a career with BBC television, directing such programmes as *Z Cars*, *The Troubleshooters* and *Sherlock Holmes*. In 1969 he became Head of BBC Television Drama.

In the 1930s the Bedford on St John's Road was a hotel, but after the Second World War it became a railway convalescent home. In the late 1950s it was taken over by the Spastic's Society (today known as SCOPE) to offer accommodation for people with cerebral palsy and related disabilities. From this time, residents at the Bedford have become very much a part of the town and are seen around, often with a carer, shopping and socialising. The Bedford also opened its doors to the town and many will remember using rooms and workshops there for further education classes.

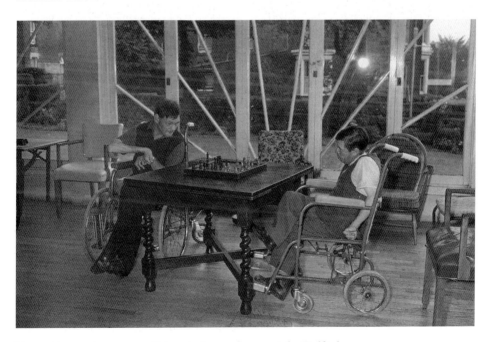

Two residents enjoy a game of chess in the sun lounge at the Bedford.

New training workshops were provided at the rear of the Bedford in the mid-1960s and can be seen here looking rather new. A number of residents are sitting out around the three-wheeler Reliant car belonging to Tommy Gunn, a resident, who worked at Otter Controls Ltd in the town.

Two residents working in the training room at the Bedford in about 1966.

three

Public Parks

Buxton has been fortunate to have been provided with good recreational facilities. In addition to Ashwood and Sylvan Parks to the east of the town, we are privileged to have one of the country's most impressive civic parks, the Pavilion Gardens. Originally gardens belonging to the adjacent Hall (now the Old Hall Hotel), the Pavilion Gardens were created when the seventh Duke of Devonshire donated twelve acres of the land to the Buxton Improvements Company who then took responsibility for the upkeep of the land. The gardens were landscaped and the glass and iron Winter Garden Pavilion was erected to the designs of Edward Milner, and the whole was opened to the public in 1871. A large concert hall designed by local architect Robert Rippon Duke was added in 1876. Here we have a view of the Pavilion Gardens' Central Hall *c.* 1920, looking eastwards. The supporting columns in the hall have been boxed in and decorated in the classic Art Nouveau style, which was prevalent at that time.

Opposite above: Another view of the Central Hall in the 1930s, showing the stylised murals bearing the town's coat of arms. Several similar murals featured on the other walls of the building

Opposite below: A view of the Concert Hall in 1938 looking westwards, adorned with Christmas bunting.

World Table Tennis Championships in February 1931, held under the dome of the Concert Hall.

Professional wrestling at the Pavilion Gardens in 1963. Popular in the 1960s and '70s , the Concert Hall hosted many bouts of the grunt 'n' groan brigade. The bouts were televised by the ITV channel and some wrestlers became popular names, including Mick McManus, Giant Haystacks, and, of course, Big Daddy, alias Shirley Crabtree.

The Central Hall of the Pavilion was part of the indoor promenade and used as a concert venue until the large concert hall opened. Here we see the interior of the Central Hall in 1970, by now known as the Lounge Bar and Restaurant. This room was rebuilt following a devastating fire in 1985, but the interior was closely modelled on the original design, with the innovative addition of a first-floor coffee shop.

Presentation time following a tennis tournament in August 1946. The winners for that year were: D.H. Slack, Gentlemen's Singles Champion of Derbyshire; Mrs Carris, Ladies' Singles Champion of Derbyshire; Mrs Carris and Mrs E.H. Harvey, Ladies' Doubles All England Championship. The wooden grandstand on the right of the picture was demolished in the 1960s because it was unsafe.

The Pavilion Gardens' rose garden. This was originally planted close to the lower lake and featured a spiral footpath leading into the centre of the plantation. The rose garden was lost many years ago but was reintroduced in the recently completed major restoration of the grounds.

Children's playground in 1932. The river Wye passes the playground and at this point is shallow enough to be used for paddling. The playground was moved to an area closer to the upper lake and completely redesigned with modern health and safety regulations in mind during the recent renovation of the gardens.

The upper lake, partially frozen over in about 1950. During particularly severe winters the lake froze over completely and was used by ice skaters. Although the lake level was lowered on these occasions to prevent tragic accidents occurring, such an amenity would never be considered in today's risk-conscious society.

A particularly overgrown view of the gardens as seen from Broad Walk in about 1934.

Croquet being played on a green in the centre of the park in the 1930s. This area today sits within the circuit of the Fun Train which runs through the central section of the gardens. Although there appears to be plenty of sunshine in this shot there are several spectators viewing the activities from the shelter of the wooden grandstand at the rear of the photograph.

A 1935 view of the tennis courts at the north-western corner of the Gardens occupying the land which is nowadays used as the car park. The building at the rear of the tennis courts, just left of centre, was used to house the Daveland Model Railway exhibition during the 1960s, which remained a popular attraction for many years.

Grass tennis courts in 1939. This area of land is now partially used as a children's playground. In the background can be seen the imposing Spa Plaza Hotel. Opened in 1866, it was originally called the Malvern House Hydropathic Hotel but was later renamed Buxton Hydropathic Ltd. In 1931, it became the Spa Hotel and was known briefly from 1938 as the Spa Plaza. In the Second World War the building was acquired by the Norwich Union Insurance Company, who evacuated their employees to Buxton for safety. After the Second World War, it ran again as the Spa Hotel until 1967, and, after closure, the hotel was demolished and the site used for warden-supported flats. These were designed by the Francis Jones Partnership for the High Peak Borough Council and built between 1973 and 1976. Known as Hartington Gardens, the flats are designed with ten bays, and to some degree imitate the original Hydropathic.

Tennis courts on Broad Walk, belonging to the Buxton Hydropathic Hotel, later the Spa Hotel. The courts occupied land previously occupied by Holly House, which had been demolished in 1925. This view dates to 1929, and today the Milton Court flats stand on this ground.

Another view of the Tennis Courts in 1929, showing the area to the north-west. Standing impressively at the rear of this shot is the short-lived Empire Hotel. Built by Spiers & Pond, it opened in 1903 but spent a very short time operating as a hotel, and ceased trading in 1914. It was used as a discharge depot for Canadian troops during the First World War, and was also in use in the Second World War. In 1946, the hotel hit the headlines when it was occupied by squatters, who were reputedly backed by the Communist Party, but they were evicted in 1949 and the hotel was demolished in 1964.

The Pavilion Gardens was not the only recreational area in Buxton. Sylvan Park and Heath Grove recreational areas had been available to the public since the late nineteenth century. Ashwood Park was laid out as a public park in 1921. This view of Ashwood Park, in 1924, shows the river Wye on the right and the bowling green on the left, which remains in use to this day.

The end of the Pavilion complex, from the Central Hall extending eastwards, has for many years been used as a conservatory housing an impressive display of plants and trees. It attracts many visitors who enjoy the floral displays. Over the years this colourful backdrop has been used for all manner of publicity events, including television productions and photographs of all kinds.

Another view of the Ashwood Park bowling green seen from across the river Wye, *c.* 1930. In the background can be seen the Midland Hotel, later to become the Ashwood Park Hotel and currently The Wye Bridge public house.

Ashwood Park looking north-west, about 1930, showing how well kept the park was with its neatly laid out lawns and flowerbeds. At the height of its popularity the park sported a well-used bandstand and attracted many visitors. Unfortunately, today it has lost its prominence in the town and would benefit from restoration.

four

Out and About with Board

The staff at Buxton Boards travelled widely in the High Peak on assignments, and, being photographers, would often stop to record good images of the majestic peak countryside. In this section, we show a mixture of commercial work and other Peak District views. Here, the old A625 winds its way around Mam Tor, known as the Shivering Mountain because of its shaley sides. Built as an alternative to the very steep gradient of Winnat's Pass, this hairpin road has now succumbed totally to the instability of the terrain on which it was built and has been closed. Here, a solitary Morris car makes its way up towards Buxton, but it is possible that the sheer weight of traffic using this road added to the tendency of the hillside to shift, thus causing its downfall. In the background, Hollins Cross can be seen to the left, Back Tor in the centre and Lose Hill to the right, a stunning backcloth for any picture.

Opposite above and below: The very distinctive hills Parkhouse and Chrome are shown in these two pictures, taken from Jericho on the back road to Earl Sterndale. Allowing for perhaps just a little widening of the road, this scene remains unaltered today, and it is likely that our photographer was here recording a good picturesque panorama.

Almost thirty miles south of Buxton at Ambergate. A very wintery but pleasant view of
the Cromford Canal as it winds its way towards Whatstandwell and Cromford. Oak Hurst
Mill chimney can be seen in the centre of the picture and Shining Cliff Woods in the right
background. The early plans to connect this canal over the White Peak with the Peak Forest Canal
at Whaley Bridge were abandoned because of the expense of locks needed to move canal traffic
over limestone terrain, a good part of which was at 350 metres above sea level. The solution was
Cromford and High Peak Railway, begun in 1826, on which the stations were called wharves.

Beyond Parkhouse and Chrome Hills is the Staffordshire Moorlands township of Longnor, once
the manor of the Harpur-Crewe family. Seen here is the Crewe and Harpur Arms Hotel, which
still serves the traveller today as it did when this postcard photograph was commissioned.

These views of the rather peaceful village of Monyash were taken for postcards and this one was the chosen card. The village green in front of the Bull's Head public house, along with children playing around the village cross and milk churns awaiting collection, make this an idyllic English village scene. The pub, having suffered for a short time the fashion of renaming, was known as The Hobbit. Thankfully, it has now returned to its original name.

This view of Monyash shows the road through, with an ancient delivery wagon going about its business. In the farmyard to the right there is a horse-drawn cart, which looks as if it was used for lime spreading.

The road out of Monyash to Parsley Hay, leaving the centre and passing the village mere or pond.

Monsal Head Viaduct looking towards Headstone Tunnel on the Midland railway line. The art critic John Ruskin was appalled to see this structure erected in the 1860s, as he thought it desecrated this delightful dale, but today the viaduct has blended into the scenery and is, indeed, seen as an important piece of industrial archaeology. How times change!

Above: Taken from the platform of the station halt at Monsal Dale, this view shows the scree-lined hills bordering the road which climbs up to Monsal Head.

Left: Looking down from the platform of the station halt at Monsal Dale, the bridge over the river Wye leads up and under the railway to ascend Putwell Hill, a very steep unmade road leading to farms on the plateau above Taddington Dale. Putwell Hill is used by cars and motorcycles competing every year in the Motorcycle Club's long running, but inappropriately named, Edinburgh Trial.

Many postcards of village scenes were produced by J.R. Board. This one is of the village of Flash, the highest village in England at 460 metres. It is shown here in the 1930s and is still a fairly isolated village today, well known for its mutual aid society, known as the Teapot Club, which still has an annual festival and parade.

The A53 Leek to Buxton road is shown here at Ramshaw Rocks. These strange outcrops, together with the neighbouring Roaches, dominate the landscape for miles. Overlooking the road on the outcrop there is a weathered shape, which looks like a face with an eye, which appears to wink as you pass it. The roadhouse and nightclub nearby, called the Winking Man, takes its name from this natural phenomenon.

Many photographs have been taken of the Cat and Fiddle Inn, perched on the summit of the Buxton to Macclesfield road at 510 metres. It is an isolated spot, often covered in mist, and is very inhospitable in the winter when snow can block the road entirely. In this view, dating to the 1930s, a charabanc is cooling down whilst its occupants have retired inside for refreshment.

View of a weathered stone formation known as Toad Rock, which stands above the A537 Buxton to Macclesfield road. It is a very aptly named gritstone outcrop.

Toad Rock showing the road below, photographed in the 1930s. There is no traffic to be seen. The photographer today would have to wait for some time for a break in the traffic to replicate this view.

The main road through Whaley Bridge, photographed just after the Second World War. The north-western bus approaches the photographer, passing the White Hart Hotel on its way to Buxton.

Whaley Bridge looking at the White Hart Hotel in about 1946. Across the road can be seen the bridge over the river Goyt.

Whaley Bridge in the late 1930s at the junction of the Buxton Road and the older turnpike road, which leads to Horwich End. The Austin Heavy 12 on the right might want to fill up at the corner petrol pump, strategically placed to catch the motorist.

At about the time this picture was taken, in the 1950s, Mr Meddins of J.R. Board photographed a large number of curbside filling stations. Perhaps this was to prepare for their eventual removal on the grounds of road safety. This is at Rowsley on the corner of the A6 road to Matlock, and the road to Chatsworth via Beeley.

A view of a well-known watering hole, the Waterloo Hotel at Taddington. Here the High Peak Hunt is assembling, with the local bobby in control in case of any traffic. Beyond the building a milk lorry loaded with milk churns can be seen, a vehicle that pre-dates the modern milk tanker. The white edging to the mudguards of the cars would suggest the date to be during or just after the Second World War. It is certainly well before the anti-hunt protesters came on the scene.

A view of the Waterloo Hotel at Taddington, showing how the building looked as you approached it from Buxton.

This view of the Waterloo Hotel at Taddington dates to the early 1950s. It would appear that the landlord has a Wolseley 4.44 car and one of his customers has a 1.5 litre Triumph sporting saloon.

Opposite above: A view of the recently removed Burbage Reservoir, looking towards the white cliffs of Grin Quarry. This spoil-heap site met travellers into Buxton from whichever direction they came. Bibbington, Grin, and Hindlow quarries all sported these unsightly tips, now thankfully removed and the land reclaimed.

Opposite below: Blackwell Mill Cottages in about 1930. They were built by the Midland Railway for signal men who operated the three-junction signal boxes in the vicinity. These were the Buxton, Peak Forest and Miller's Dale junction boxes. This was not an easy place to live: there were no shops for miles around. The main way of travelling was to walk to Topley Pike and catch a bus, or use the unique small station at Blackwell Mill, provided as a halt by the railway company and at which trains stopped, by request, on certain days only. Above the cottages can be seen the central works, with the quarry and a raft of empty rail wagons with the Buxton Lime Firm's initials.

The Bull i' th' Thorn Inn on the A515, formerly Hurdlow House, is a very old coaching inn still welcoming the traveller today. Here, in the 1930s, visitors gathered for the nearby Flagg point-to-point races.

Flagg Races, held in the 1930s on the Tuesday after Easter Monday, were frequently affected by the snow and bad weather, but this had no noticeable affect on the drinking! In this view, at the The Bull i' th' Thorn Inn, many coach loads of racegoers have arrived. In the foreground are three Austin 10s, two from about 1935 and one from about 1938. The Wolseley is perhaps a 12 or 14hp of about 1936.

The bar is no doubt rather crowded at the The Bull i' th' Thorn Inn, and no drink and driving law is in force. A Ford 8 Y-Type is parked at a slightly rakish angle, alongside the Austin 12hp, which has a D-shaped split rear window.

five

Local
Commerce

The firm of J.R. Board took many photographs of businesses in the High Peak to be used for publicity purposes. In this section we show the wide range of work undertaken. This action shot shows the occasional dangerous situation the photographer would find himself in. The limestone quarry face is being shot-fired to bring down the stone for crushing. The sequence of limestone processing photographs which follow were taken in October 1967, at the Lime Sand Mortar Ltd works at Dove Holes Dale.

Here is the quarry face after blasting. The stone will be transported to the crusher as a first step in processing.

The firm Lime Sand Mortar was a subsidiary of S. Taylor Frith & Co. Ltd, whose works were in Dove Holes Dale between Peak Dale and Dove Holes. Lime Sand Mortar Ltd made a lime-based plaster used in the building trade for interior wall finishing. The first Limelite plant was set up in Pontypridd in 1965, but at the time of these photographs, in 1967, manufacture had moved to the works of Taylor Frith at Dove Holes Dale. Here, limelite backing plaster is being bagged and palletised, ready for storage and despatch from the warehouse.

A view of the bagging plant showing the hopper feeds to the automatic sack fillers, and the forklift truck ready to move a full pallet. The livery of the delivery lorries was cream with the slogan 'Serving British Builders – L.S.M.' in red on the sides. Of its many uses in building, it is known that houses in Sherbrook Grove, Buxton, were plastered with Limelite.

In the 1960s, John Meddins of J.R. Board went out to the firm of J. Thornhill & Sons Ltd at Great Longstone near Bakewell. Here is shown the offices and factory of the firm supplying eggs and oven-ready poultry.

The Egg Marketing Board's old slogan 'Go to work on an egg' is evoked by this picture of the eggs being graded and packed.

Everyone is busy grading and sorting eggs at the Derbyshire Egg Station in Great Longstone.

Delivery of oven-ready poultry and eggs direct to the shop.

The long-running firm IXL Laundry began life at Laundry Cottages, Fairfield, before moving to Charles Street, Buxton, firstly to premises which later became the bus garage, and finally to a purpose-built laundry in 1915, which was extended in 1922. The laundry, adjacent to the railway bridge, was demolished in 2004. This photograph shows the press room where laundry was finished on rotary presses.

The machinery in the wash house was taken out in the early 1960s and replaced with industrial washing machines.

The industrial washing machines, photographed here in February 1968, look just like a large version of the front-loading machine found in the average kitchen.

A very modern plant was installed in the 1960s, which provided efficiency and savings on staff. The calender machine sheet ironer, operating over three rollers, was run by three staff.

The IXL shop in Spring Gardens, taken in May 1968. It was opened by the famous disc jockey and television personality Jimmy Saville.

After the Second World War, the government gave large subsidies to farmers to help to increase agricultural output. Up to seventy per cent of the cost of liming the land could be reclaimed, so there was a call for lime spreaders. Due to the unavailability of new vehicles these lime spreaders were fabricated using ex-War Department vehicles. In this workshop at the Stud Farm, Waterswallows Road, Fairfield, half-track and other vehicles were converted. This shows the engineers and fitters in April 1951.

A half-track converted for lime spreading use in 1951. The conversion was not entirely successful, however, because the vehicle had been originally designed for use in the desert, and after conversion there was a tendency for the drive tracks to sheer on the harsher Peak District terrain.

A converted Chevrolet lorry with spreading equipment at the rear. Though a four-wheel drive lorry, the weight of lime carried was kept quite modest, so that the lorry did not get bogged down in the farmer's field.

Another view of the workshops at the Stud Farm, Waterswallows Road, taken in 1951. The building later became a store for Brake Linings Ltd until houses were built on the site in the 1980s.

Although tankers were in use by the lime companies, the firm of J. Ripley Ltd, of Long Lane, Chapel-en-le-Frith, provided the first bulk-powder tanker for private hire in the area. The Seddon Diesel 71 JRA, seen here in about 1958, was fitted with an ALC tank and Welworthy blower and equipment. The photograph is taken at Long Lane garage which is now part of the haulage firm of Somersets Ltd.

After the Second World War, new vehicles were in short supply and ex-War Department vehicles were converted to private commercial use. The firm of T. Rowbotham, who had a garage on the corner of Crossings Road in Chapel-en-le-Frith, converted a number of Chevrolet lorries, and here is a Chevrolet used by the New Mills Co-operative Society. The four-figure telephone number suggests a post-war date, but the lorry still has wartime headlamps and white-edged mudguards.

A Chevrolet converted for Charles Mason & Co. by Rowbotham's Garage. Charles Mason & Co. were wholesale grocers and provision merchants of Chesterfield who supplied hotels and restaurants in the High Peak.

This Chevrolet, in use by Z. & W. Wade of Whaley Bridge, has been fitted with a tipping body by the firm of Edbro of Bolton, and is using a single tipper ram. It is seen here in Whaley Bridge near the wharf yard.

This Seddon Diesel was probably supplied to the haulier Philip Heyworth by Rowbotham's Garage in the early 1950s. It is on contract to E. & F. Beattie Ltd. The haulage depot of Heyworth Bros was at the garage on the Glossop Road at Chapel Milton, opposite the Crown & Mitre Hotel, just under the railway bridge.

Newfield Garage of Lomas Bros Ltd, motor engineers and coach builders, was on the road between Chapel-en-le-Frith and Whaley Bridge, at Tunstead Milton. It is shown here after the firm changed to Regent Fuels and the pumps had been re-sited. Lomas Bros were agents for Vauxhall cars, such as the one shown at the pump, and Bedford commercial vehicles. Lomas Bros also ran the Wren Nest Garage at Glossop and the Spa Garage, Market Place, Buxton.

Most likely supplied by Lomas Bros, these seven ambulances have been joined by two Austin taxis, which were also used in the 1950s for transporting patients. The line-up is in a field near to the Lomas Bros Garage. The two smaller ambulances are the same design as the Bedford Dormobile mobile caravan, whilst the larger Bedford ambulances were purpose built from the 1950s.

All businesses need a bank and the banks also commissioned J.R. Board for publicity photographs. Here is the interior of the Westminster Bank at Chapel-en-le-Frith. In the foreground is a Burroughs calculating machine, the forerunner of today's computer.

The exterior of the Westminster Bank at Chapel-en-le-Frith.

Two views of the Williams Deacon's Bank at Cavendish Circus, Buxton. J.R. Board's premises is just a few shops up the circus from this bank. Judging by the Rover car, this shot dates from the late 1940s. Note the colonnading is carried through the whole length of Cavendish Circus.

A 1960s view of the Williams Deacon's Bank at Cavendish Circus, the colonnading has now disappeared. The bank building was adapted for banking purposes by local architects Bryden & Walton at a cost of over £3,400 in 1909. Formerly the Sheffield & Rotherham Bank, the business had become Williams Deacon's by 1912.

From the late 1940s, the Milk Marketing Board ran an artificial insemination centre at Brook House, Fairfield. Here is shown the exterior south front of the old house which served as offices: the picture was taken in June 1949. During the Second World War, it was used as accommodation for army officers.

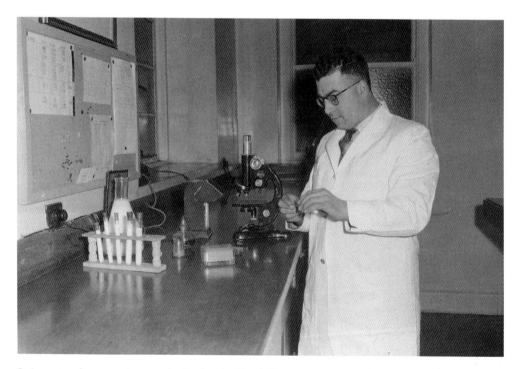

Stringent quality control was maintained at the Brook House centre. Here the chemist is carrying out a milk test in 1949.

Right and below: For artificial insemination purposes, fine bulls were kept at the farm at Brook House. Here, two bull handlers pose their majestic animals for the camera in January 1957.

This view of Brook House, taken in June 1949, shows the magnificent setting of the Milk Marketing Board centre, with Blake Edge rising to 507 metres in the background.

R.B. Morten, the Buxton Creamery, was established in 1887 and had premises in Green Lane. The company also opened a shop at 115 Victoria Park Road, Fairfield, which was a dairy and a milk bar using the 1960s slogan, 'Drinka pinta milka day'.

The milk counter of Morten's Dairy at 115 Victoria Park Road, in about 1968.

The grocery counter of Morten's Dairy at 115 Victoria Park Road, in about 1968.

From the mid-1960s right through the 1970s, the Barbecue Restaurant specialised in Scotch Angus steaks and also offered casino facilities at 25 Spring Gardens. One of their areas of business expansion was ice cream making. These three photographs were most likely taken for publicity purposes. The caravan is ready to serve dairy farm ice cream.

Opposite above: In 1958, when the shopping arcade was opened on Victoria Park Road, Fairfield, most people still used the local shops for their food and everyday items. In addition to the dairy and grocer there was a cake shop, a newsagent, a hardware store, a post office and other retailers.

Opposite below: Ice cream making in the model ice cream dairy in Spring Gardens.

A young customer is served from the ice cream kiosk.

six

Education

The Board collection contains photographs of Buxton's secondary schools. There were two
state schools for boys: Kents Bank Secondary Modern and Buxton College Grammar School.
Silverlands Secondary Modern and Cavendish Grammar School provided education for the town's
girls. In addition to the state schools, the town also had a number of private schools, including the
Normanton Private Boarding and Day School, on St Johns Road, founded in the 1930s. Before
this the building was occupied by another private school, St Michael's Preparatory. At the time of
this photograph, the school was exclusively for boys but later on admitted girls.

The Normanton School shared its building with the Buxton Sea Cadets. This shot shows the
flagpole where the cadets' colours could be hoisted.

A cricket match on the playing fields, Normanton School.

The gymnasium at the Normanton School was built in 1927 when the school was still known as St Michael's.

Domestic Science class, Cavendish Girls' School, in the 1930s.

Opposite above: Normanton School. This image can be dated pretty firmly to the 1960s when the fashion of teaching languages in a language laboratory was in vogue. The teacher could listen in to each individual student as he read a prepared text. This technique was considered to be very advanced at the time.

Opposite below: Science class, Cavendish Girls' School, in about 1950. Note how the lights over the benches can be lowered or raised on a counterbalancing weight.

A class posing for the camera at St Anne's Catholic School in the 1950s.

The open side doors in this shot indicate fine weather outside. The boys, however, are still wearing their blazers, which was a rule firmly adhered to at the Buxton College. Exceptionally high temperatures occasionally triggered relaxation of this rule, but only with the express permission of the presiding teacher, who never removed his academic gown regardless of the weather. In this way, the student was trained to be a stiff-upper-lipped Englishman!

Buxton College, showing the newly built Widdows blocks which enclosed a quadrangle of open land in the middle. By the 1920s, class accommodation was becoming a problem and this new block, completed in 1929, went some way to solving this problem.

The new extensions to the Wesleyan Sunday School, Fountain Street, shortly after completion in 1938.

The celebration of Whitsuntide, seven weeks after Easter, commemorates the descent of the Holy Ghost upon the Apostles, who were inspired to preach the Christian Gospels. In the Roman Catholic church, a Walk of Witness takes place on Whitsunday. Here are children from the Roman Catholic school.

A view of the Catholic Schools' Whitsunday Walk, which is passing the Thermal Baths on the way up Terrace Road to the church of St Anne.

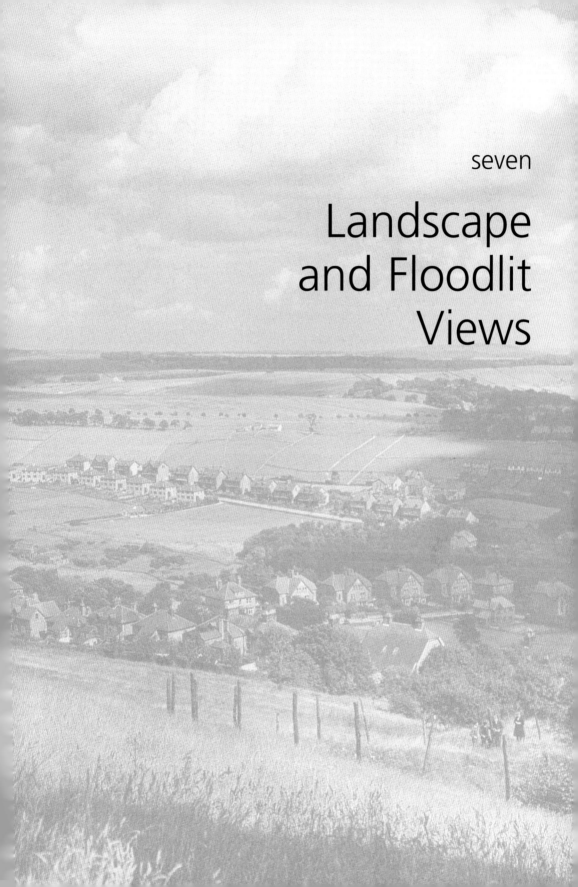

seven

Landscape
and Floodlit
Views

Lower Buxton in the 1930s. The local bus is seen here next to Turner's Memorial, in front of the Hot Baths. As can be seen from this shot, there is very little vehicular traffic, and, of course, no need for traffic lights, which did not arrive in Buxton until the 1960s. The accepted way of controlling traffic at a busy crossroads like this was by the use of a traffic policeman, who can be seen here in operation in the left foreground.

A high-level view of the Crescent and bottom of Terrace Road, showing the bus in the same place as the previous picture. By the look of the flag at half mast on the Crescent's east wing, it seems that this photograph coincided with a national tragedy or bereavement.

A view of The Slopes and a glimpse of Higher Buxton, taken from the roof of the Crescent, *c.* 1930. To the left of this view is the spire of the Congregational church. Built in 1861, the church was designed by the Duke of Devonshire's architect, Henry Currey, and built by local builder Robert R. Duke. It was demolished in 1983. The large buildings seen on the right horizon are the Peak Buildings, which, by the time of this photograph, were being used to house the town's museum and public library.

A view of The Slopes, showing the formally laid out paths and carefully planted trees. The Town Hall, opened in 1889 and designed by Manchester architect William Pollard, can be seen at the top of this view. St Ann's Well is seen at the bottom of this view, still sporting its pepper-pot domes at each end of the roof. These were later deemed to be unsafe and were removed in 1937. The chimney in the top right belonged to the Spa Laundry which was a part of the Spa Hotel.

Every town has a favoured vantage point for photography and this is Buxton's. Over the years, literally thousands of photographs of the town have been taken from the roof of the Town Hall, which is easily the highest point within the Buxton basin. This shot shows the Devonshire Hospital, the Palace Hotel, the Crescent, the Quadrant and, interestingly, the two separate railway stations on the right of the picture. Both built to the same design, the one on the left was the London & North-Western Railway and the one on the right was the Midland Railway.

Opposite above: In the fifty years from 1849, no fewer than eleven churches or chapels were built in Buxton. In this view, looking north east from the slopes, three can be seen. The Congregational church of 1861 is on the left and we have a good view of the 1861 St Anne's Catholic church on the right. In the middle background can be seen the tower of the Trinity church on Hardwick Mount, built 1873.

Opposite below: Expansion in Buxton can be seen in the middle foreground, which shows the relatively new development of the Brown Edge Road, on high ground to the north east of the main town, about 1935.

The town, photographed from high ground on Corbar Hill, *c.* 1935. The undeveloped nature of Fairfield can be clearly seen on the left of this view. Victoria Park Road can be seen leading into Fairfield but it seems that at the time of this photograph only Overdale and Milnbank Avenues have been built. A good view of the Spring Gardens' viaduct can be seen on the left.

The fields behind Green Lane in 1930. Behind the trees on the left are the playing fields belonging to Buxton College. This view was taken from high ground at the base of Grin Woods.

A 1930 view of the area to the north of the town, which until recently was the site of Lightwood Reservoir.

From the late 1930s to the early 1960s it was fashionable to illuminate the Pavilion Gardens in the evenings, and it became a regular family attraction to tour the gardens lit in various colours. Here we see the official switching on the lights.

Pavilion Gardens promenade with lights in the tree branches. The central hall of the pavilion and large concert hall to the right are well lit.

Opposite above: Illuminated stretch of the river Wye and bridge, looking westwards, *c.* 1930. The wrought-iron bridge was part of the 1871 layout of the gardens by Edward Milner.

Opposite below: Pavilion Gardens bridge and promenade. The reflection of the lighting in the river Wye below the bridge is very effective.

In addition to the Pavilion Gardens, many of the town's prominent buildings were given the 'Son et Lumiere' treatment. The Devonshire Hospital, Palace Hotel and Crescent are lit to good effect in this shot.

Isolated by surrounding darkness, the Palace Hotel is bathed in projected light in 1960.

Right: Despite its relative isolation on the Slopes, the town's war memorial did not escape the illuminations. More recently, after the renovation of the Slopes, the war memorial has been permanently lit at night.

Below: The Pavilion Gardens to the left, and Old Hall Hotel in the 1930s.

At ground level the effect of the lighting is emphasised through the arches of the Crescent. This photograph was taken in 1939.

eight

High Peak Water

The reputation of Buxton is built on its natural mineral water, which emerges from springs in the Crescent at a constant temperature of 82 degrees Fahrenheit (27.5 degrees Celsius). The firm of J.R Board took many photographs of the Buxton baths but also travelled out of town to record other watery scenes. In this section we show some rare images of the Buxton Baths and Clinic, but the section begins with views of rather more prosaic uses of water. Here is a view of Errwood Reservoir in the Goyt Valley, taken in about 1970. If you dont fancy the exertion of sailing you can always take a picnic and watch others on the water!

A good view of sailing on the Errwood Reservoir in about 1966.

At the top of Lightwood Road in Buxton was a small reservoir, seen here looking towards the town.

A rephotographed image from the early part of the twentieth century, showing sheep dipping in the Hogshaw Brook at the junction of Brown Edge and Lightwood Roads. Entrance to Brown Edge Road was over a ford until 1920, when a small concrete girder bridge with a 15ft wide carriageway and a 5ft wide footpath was erected across the stream.

The Tonic Bath at the bottom of Bath Road Walk offered cold bathing, with a water temperature of between 60 and 68 degrees Fahrenheit (15.4 and 20 degrees Celsius), and it had a rather chequered commercial history for 200 years from the 1770s. Between 1862 and 1864, the Devonshire Buxton Estate made considerable improvements to the bath and covered it with a semi-circular roof. This re-photographed earlier image dates to about 1875: the house to the right is Bath House and behind this can be seen part of the roof of the bath. The terrace of houses in the background, Broad Walk, are very new, having been built between 1861 and 1875.

Left: The entrance and interior hall after the 1924 remodelling. The floors were paved with black and white marble and the walls were lined with Carrara Arni-vein marble and Kerry-red marble bands to produce a very stylish interior.

Below: In 1924 the Natural Baths underwent extensive remodelling when the entrance was moved to the centre of the front facade. Here is shown the Natural Baths' front in a photograph used in the conference brochure of the early 1930s.

The large Gentlemens' Public Bath in about 1924. The attendant has a water douche for spray treatments. This bath was in constant use from the time of the Romans to its final closure in 1972. It is now foreshortened and covered with a dome, in order to provide controlled conditions for the water to be taken for bottling by the Buxton Mineral Water Company.

The Ladies' Public Bath, seen here in about 1924, was designed by Henry Currey for the 1851-4 rebuild of the baths. It remains today, still with many of its original features.

After bathing treatment, the patient would spend time relaxing in the cooling room. This room, dating to 1924, is today the Tourist Information Centre, though, sadly, the panelling does not remain.

At the east end of the Crescent, the Thermal Baths are shown here in about 1928. The new colonnading, with electric light, was erected in 1909-10 to the designs of local architects Bryden and Walton. The Morris Cowley tourer is able to park in an uncluttered street! (On page eighty-five of volume one of *Buxton* from the Board Collection, we show a similar view taken at the same time. Readers may like to spot the difference!)

Here we see an overhead view of the St Anne's Well, taken in about 1930. It is interesting to note that the roads are still made of crushed limestone: very dusty in dry conditions. This photograph gives a good view of the Grove Hotel and the end of Spring Gardens.

Right: In 1935, a group of businessmen exploited a niche in the market by opening a clinic for patients described as middle class but with moderate means. The Buxton Clinic Ltd was at the east end of the Crescent, and patients received their water treatment in the adjacent Thermal Baths. Here we see the covered walkway between clinic and baths. Today there is, between the Thermal Baths and the east end of the Crescent, a narrow passageway where the wall of the outside of the Thermal Baths is built of white glazed bricks. If anyone has wondered why an exterior wall should be glazed in this way, here is the answer.

Below: The physiotherapy room in the Buxton Clinic in about 1938, ready for the patient. The physio' table is in the centre, and gymnasium bars and a forerunner of the Zimmer frame can be see in the background, whilst in the foreground is an autoclave for sterilisation purposes.

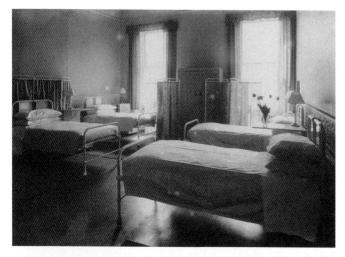

The patient might be accommodated in a small ward at the clinic in 1938, though, for the more affluent, a single bedroom could be provided.

Relaxation facilites after a hard day of hydrotherapy in the clinic included this lounge and snooker room.

It is likely that this lift was provided for the Buxton Clinic in the 1930s. It was situated in the east entrance of the Crescent and positioned so as to mask architect John Carr's impressive cantilevered staircase leading to the Assembly Room. Thankfully, it has now gone, removed during the extensive refurbishment of the east wing of the Crescent by the Derbyshire County Council between 1970 and 1975.

Above and below: Rehabilitation, exercise and remedial games taking place in the Natural Baths. The men are actually using the Ladies' Public Bath, though it may be that in 1947, when this picture was taken, the distinction between pools in the Natural Baths was not observed. It is possible that these are ex-armed forces personnel, undergoing rehabilitation at Buxton.

After closure in September 1963 the Thermal Baths lay empty, apart from occasional use by local groups, until 1986 when the building opened as the Cavendish shopping arcade. In March 1966 the BBC asked J.R. Board for photographs of the interior. Here is one of the main corridors showing doors to the small consultation rooms leading off.

Gentlemen's corridor of the Thermal Baths in 1966, with former treatment rooms to the left.

The cooling room of the Thermal Baths in 1966.

The corridor of the Thermal Baths in 1966. It is interesting to compare these interior views with the layout of the present Cavendish Arcade, where it will be seen that many of the glazed Minton tiles have been kept *in situ* and others replaced, in keeping with originals. In the shopping arcade today there are very good interpretation boards telling the story of the baths, and a large plunge bath and a smaller bath have been preserved.

An interesting view of John Carr's magnificent Assembly Room in the Buxton Crescent, completed in about 1784 with stunning fibrous plaster ceiling work and a clever symmetrical room design. Once used for very grand dress balls and assemblies, its use here in 1938 is rather more prosaic – as a dining room for the Buxton Clinic.

nine

Buxton
Weather

Turner's memorial, arguably the town centre, has been photographed here after a moderate fall of snow. The North-Western Roadcar Company's bus is loading up with passengers. All the town services, except those which started at the station, used this stop in all directions, thus allowing passengers the comfort of standing under the Thermal Baths' arcade. In the foreground, an ex-War Department Bedford lorry belonging to J.R. Lomas is doing the rounds, delivering coal. These were very extensive at this time of the year in Buxton: in fact, all the coal merchants in town were run off their feet as demand rose with the arrival of the very bad weather. In this picture also are some contemporary cars; a very new-looking Sunbeam Talbot, of about 1955, outside the baths, gives an approximate date to this view. This view also shows an Austin 10 or 12 of 1948 and an earlier Morris 8 Tourer dating to 1935, between the bus and the lorry. The bus JA 7729 was built in 1938 with a Bristol LG5 engine and an Eastern Counties' Carriage Works body. In 1952, it was re-bodied by the firm of Willowbrook and had the fleet number 829. The bus had seen many Buxton winters when it was finally withdrawn from service in 1961.

Opposite above: Judging by the depth of snow on the seat in the foreground, a fall of some 8 or 10in (20-25cm) of snow has just taken place. St John's church looks very picturesque within this snowy scene. As usual, roads and pavements have been cleared and people are able to move about with reasonable convenience. The only dating clue to this picture is the rather distant Series 1 Land Rover heading towards the photographer on St John's Road. This vehicle is one of the 10in chassis types introduced in 1954, so this picture could be from the mid-1950s.

Opposite below: A very fine snow scene, looking towards Burlington Road from the Serpentine.

Heatherton on Temple Road, built for Manchester stockbroker Henry Lancashire in 1912, seen here after a good fall of snow. It was occupied by Thomas Neilson Brown of the Manchester departmental store Aflick and Brown in the 1930s, and was renamed Hartington House in 1953, becoming part of the Buxton College. It is now divided into apartments and known as Temple Court.

Postal workers, like other delivery personnel, have it very rough indeed during bad winters. Carrying bags of mail to Fairfield, Ladmanlow and Harpur Hill was bad enough in good weather, but in conditions like these it was very hard work indeed. Here the photographer has stepped across the road from his shop in the Cavendish Colonnade to the post office at the top of the Quadrant, where the post office management publicly thanks the workers for their efforts.

Traffic waits patiently at the top of Fairfield Road for the snow ploughs to do their work over Fairfield Common. Even though the snow fall looks only moderate in depth, the winds will, no doubt, have raised a good few drifts between here and the village of Dove Holes. Ideal weather conditions, perhaps, for the Adams Butter van to be stuck in. This firm, originating in Leek, was taken over by the Irish Milk Marketing Board, and Adams' butter, spreading everywhere, changed to Kerrygold.

A rather desolate Palace Hotel closed to business in bad weather conditions, which could very soon have caused severe damage in a building of this size. The picture, taken probably in 1979 by Mr Turner, shows the hotel closed and no admittance allowed. Luckily, for both the hotel and the town, new owners were quickly forthcoming and it would again take its place as one of Buxton's foremost hotels.

The photographer's car is seen here on the road from the Wanted Inn at Sparrowpit to Mam Tor and Winnat's Pass. He apparently stopped his car and walked back to get this shot of the Dark Peak features in winter.

For some, the arrival of snow is not a season to look forward to. Farmers and their livestock certainly suffer difficult times. Finding and getting food to the animals can prove very hazardous.

Despite the depth of snow and great freeze-up in 1947 Buxton managed to stagger on, but the terrible effect that ice had on the exposed power lines was the final straw. Many areas were without electricity for weeks. This picture shows the *War of the Worlds* effect on the pylons: their heads bent over rather like H.G. Wells' invaders from space. Mr Meddins, of J.R. Board, photographed many of these structures for the Electricity Board. This view is towards the Waterswallows sub-station.

Ashwood Dale in the snow. An ex-Midland railway six-coupled goods engine heads towards Buxton, with, more than likely, a good few loads of coal destined for the merchants in the Higher Buxton coal yard. It is interesting to recall that in the 1940s and '50s, when this photograph was taken, the bulk of the coal was conveyed by rail. Many people relied on coal for the only heat in their house and expected the coal merchant to deliver when required. The merchants in turn ordered vast quantities from the coal mines, keeping them turning out more and more of the stuff. Stockpiling was obviously necessary to help cover the periods of bad weather but the amazing thing was that it all worked like clockwork.

Above: J.R. Board often copied older photographs onto a glass plate negative – this is one. It shows well how snow ploughing was done before the advent of the lorry-mounted plough. Here we see the 1hp model climbing Cheese Hill towards the Market Place, and some of the older buildings which formerly fronted this road can also be seen.

Right: Here is a group of singers braving the weather outside the George Hotel whilst the photographer keeps warm and dry inside the hotel entrance!

Opposite: Whilst the wintery weather made life very difficult for the adults, it was a source of great fun and exercise for the youngsters, who would head for the many places in town good for sledging. Here we see tobogganing, called sledging in Buxton, taking place in Palace Fields, a favourite spot for children of this area. Note also that the pavements of Lightwood Road are cleared for pedestrians.

Other local titles published by Tempus

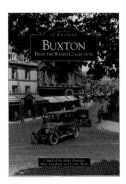

Buxton From the Board Collection
MIKE BENTLEY, MIKE LANGHAM, COLIN WELLS

This collection of over 200 old images of Buxton draws on the archive of photographs deposited on its closure by the J.R. Board company to the Buxton Museum in the 1970s. The photographs offer a unique insight into the life and times of Buxton during the first half of the twentieth century.

0 7524 1586 7

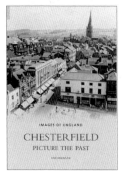

Chesterfield Picture the Past
ANN KRAWSZIK

This collection of over 200 old photographs of Chesterfield is a sample of the many thousands of images which are now available to view on the award-winning website www.picturethepast.org.uk. These images, many never before published, provide a fascinating pictorial history of Chesterfield over the past 150 years. The result is a book that will delight anyone who has lived or worked in this popular market town with the leaning spire.

0 7524 3581 7

Derbyshire in the 1930s A Lantern Slide Journey
ARTHUR ROOKSBY AND DONALD ROOKSBYR

This beautiful book of photographs takes the reader through some of the most scenic parts of Derbyshire as they looked in the inter-war years. Pastoral scenes of farmland and dale follow views of towns and villages, and the county town itself, all looking quieter and calmer than they do today. The photographs were all taken originally to be used as lantern slides to entertain audiences in village halls around the county.

0 7524 3258 3

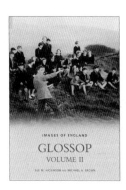

Glossop Volume two
SUE HICKSON & MICHAEL BROWN

This fascinating collection of over 200 images portrays life in and around the Derbyshire town of Glossop over the last 100 years. There were many photographic studios in the area producing picture postcards featuring idyllic rural scenes, mills, shops, civic events and celebrations. Accompanied by informative captions, this volume will be of interest to all those who have lived and worked in the area, or who have spent time exploring the valleys and dales of north Derbyshire.

0 7524 3286 9

If you are interested in purchasing other books published by Tempus, or in case you have difficulty finding any Tempus books in your local bookshop, you can also place orders directly through our website
www.tempus-publishing.com